GIANI SANT SINGH MASKEEN

ISHWAR SINGH

Made with ♥ on the Notion Press Platform
www.notionpress.com

I am dedicating this book to the great religious preacher of Sikhism Giani Sant Singh Ji Maskeen.

Contents

Foreword

Ishwar Singh have more than ten years of experience in writing story books, sakhis of devotional saints and in research activities. He is a tremendous writer. He is doing excellent job by writing about Giani Sant Singh Maskeen. He had shown very keen interest in the field of religious resources and other cultural issues.

He is also a very excellent teacher and also having deep knowledge about the social science issues. I have always seen him working very hard for his various books. He just want to express about the Indian culture to our new generations in a simple and brief manner. I wish him all the very best for his new book.

Birinder Pal Kaur

Preface

This book is about the brief history of Giani Sant Singh Maskeen. The task behind to publish such content is to spread knowledge about the unsung heroes of the Sikh history among the new generation. In the schools, which are being organised by Sikh trusts, the students are just getting very limited knowledge about the Sikh warriors. Baba Banda Singh Bahadur, Baba Deep Singh etc. are the common names on the tongues of the students but they don't know about the others. This is just an effort to spread this brief information among new generations. I hope that you will like this book.

Acknowledgements

Writing a book is harder than I thought and more rewarding than I could have ever imagined. None of this would have been possible without my best friend, my teacher, my best motivator, my beloved mother Amarjit Kaur. She was the first who inspired me for my goals and taught me various subjects and created my interest specially in Social Sciences. She stood by me during every struggle and all my successes. Whatever I had achieved in my life it is due to my mother.

I'm eternally grateful to my father Pal Singh, who took in an extra mouth to feed when he didn't have to. He taught me discipline, tough love, manners, respect, and so much more that has helped me succeed in life. I truly have no idea where I'd be if he hadn't given me a roof over my head whom I desperately needed at that age.

To my father-in-law Narinder Singh for their moral support during the up and downs in my life. He taught me how to live positive even in the worst situations by sharing his personal experiances. He is the man who suggest me to write a book in your life because it will be your book by which you will be remembered in future.

Finally, to all those who have been a part of my getting there: Sukhbir Singh, Jarnail Singh, Beant Kaur, Devinder Kumar Sharma, Sumeet Kaur, Rinkpal Singh and Iqbal Singh.

Prologue

India is a country of huge cultural diversities. This diversity has its roots in the ancient and medieval period of the history. In present day life, every one is playing his role according to the role assingned by the nature. I have very much interest to explore various great warriors or personalities and cultural aspects of our Indian Society. So an idea came in my mind to explore the brief history of Giani Sant Singh Maskeen. In this book, I have focused on the various achievements of Giani Sant Singh Maskeen. I am writing this book for our younger generations so that when they will read this book, they must understand the sacrifices and struggles of our forefathers.

CHAPTER ONE

Giani Sant Singh Maskeen

Giani Sant Singh Maskeen (1934–2005) was raised in 1934 in the Pakistani region of Bannu at a village named Lak Marwat. Giani ji, the sole child of his mom and dad, spent the 57 years of his life in Alwar, Rajasthan.

Maskeen Ji seemed to be extremely lucky to stay alive, by God's kindness, and eventually settled in Alwar, Rajasthan, along with vast numbers of numerous different Sikhs who have been forcibly removed from one`s native lands all through the uncontrolled depiction of one country into two in 1947. That saw the mass killings of uncountable millon of men, women, and young kids. A Religious function has indeed been organized annually beneath his close oversight on the first, second, and third of March for the previous 40 years. Renowned gurmat academics and lecturers, Kirtan Jathas, along with hundreds of admirers from all across the nation, have travelled to attend in the yearly religious functions.

According to Sikh custom, the unrestricted communal food known as was open for 3 days and fed to anybody whoever arrived. Such occasions in Alwar featured extraordinary interactions and frequently well-attended.

Several areas surrounding Alwar township have a little Sikh community. Underneath the capable leadership of Maskeen Ji, two Sikh institutes are currently operational, and a sizable academic facility had previously been built. Such social improvement initiatives' future and execution are currently of severe importance.

The mom and dad of Giani Ji were Mata Ram Kaur and Sardar Kartar Singh. Maskeen Ji's elementary schooling was at the Sikh Academy, but the turbulence of Division of India prevented him from finishing his secondary schooling at Govt High School. According to the founder of the nation, Mohammad Ali Jinnah, who envisioned secular Pakistan for individuals of all faiths and ideologies, his family was lucky excessively to dodge the genocides of Muslim crowds who desired their newborn "Land of the Pure" devoid of anybody who wasn't really Muslim.

Maskeen ji's pain for his family members' mental suffering by his own words:

"It was past midnight one day. Sister and parents were all sound asleep. My parents were sleeping when I knelt at their feet and exited the house. After I departed, I imagined that my parents would be devastated. I also understood that the sacrifice I made for my father would cause him to hurt and cry, but what can I do when I am also in pain and crying? Such emotional suffering at such a young age rendered me completely useless. A sister will get humbled if she is proud of her only brother. My mental suffering would weigh more than that of my family if I were to weigh this mental suffering. I boarded the Delhi-bound passenger train at early morning, and after six and a half to seven hours, I arrived there. As soon as I arrived in Delhi, I went to Gurdwara Sis Ganj to send my greetings and to the ascetic and baragi Satguru Teg Bahadurji to deposit my problems. After praying, I left the building. I just had 12 rupees on me. I boarded the bus for Bharatpur and arrived at the Gurdwara after purchasing a three rupee ticket. An elderly scribe from the Gurdwara used to fervently and continuously recite Satnam Sri Waheguru. I knelt at their knees and cried out, "Baba Ji!" I have three to four days to remain here. They began uttering "live joyfully." There was a brief evening satsang. Granthi Singh read each word aloud. Kirtan Sohila was recited before entering Maharaj Ji's Sukh-Asana. It was then finished. Have you drank the langar water, Granthi Singh said as he approached his home. I spoke without thinking, Babaji. What region are you from? I declared, "I've arrived at Delhi." They concluded that I hadn't eaten since the morning based on the appearance of my face. A langar was prepared for a visitor whenever he arrived at the temple; otherwise, none was prepared. In Langri Singh's opinion, I still hadn't arrived and neither had any passengers today. At the past, Baba Ji lived alone in the Gurdwara. They offered me two parshadas and vegetables from the four they had saved for themselves in the langar. After eating the two parshadas, I slept off. At dawn, I rose, bathed, and prayed to the Lord, the giver. Please let me know what future holds. Give me a task that takes into account how I'm feeling. Because I was aware that my thoughts would not rest anyplace, I also understood that whatever I was requesting was the incorrect thing. O Akal Purukh, I asked for it! Bind my feet to yours. Granthi Babaji started saying that son after I remained in the Gurdwara for three days! Only three days are allowed for visitors to remain here. When Pradhan Sahib arrives in the evening, you can only extend your stay by requesting it from him. Babaji, I exclaimed. No need to inquire; I go on. I was astonished at the time when Babaji's eyes started to get moist upon knowing me, as if we had a shared history. I will always remember the moment Babaji's eyes started to become moist as I left."

The struggle days of Maskeen Ji at the religious places of the great industrial city of Bombay by his own words:

"I arrived in Bombay while sitting in the train without a ticket. I left Dadar station and made my way on foot to Dadar Gurdwara after avoiding T.T's sight. I did a little nitnam by having a chilly tap water bath. I was famished. I questioned Granthi Singh if langar was prepared here. They began claiming that this is the Sri Guru Singh Sabha Gurudwara; langar is not conducted here. Granthi ji began remarking that Kohliwara was somewhat distant from here. There are a total of two or three Gurdwaras. In a Gurdwara, the langar is prepared. I boarded the electric train at Dadar station and travelled to Bombay after completely questioning Granthi Singh. I arrived at the Gurdwara and it was stated there that Langar would only be accessible for three days and not after that. Well! I used to spend the day wandering the streets and spend the evenings sitting at the Gurdwara. I used to take langar at the appropriate time. The third day, Langri Singh rudely informed me that it was my third day. I used to go without a ticket on the electric train. I made it to Kohliwara. I learned some tricks, including how to board a train without a ticket and how to hide from T.T. When I arrived at the Kohliwade Gurdwara, I saw that langar is strictly enforced there as well. After three days of langar, a man who appeared to be the leader of that Gurdwara began telling me in a very severe manner that Bhai Sahib, this is not an orphanage, it is a Gurudwara. Make your other plans because you have been at this place for three days. There was a Gurdwara nearby called Guru Nanak's Durbar at Sindhi Kani. There was a kirtan that day for Bibi Tilly Bai, a well-known Sindhi at the time. Numerous folks had shown up. I also showed up. There was a sizable corporation there. Giani Gurdayal Singh served as the court scribe in that time. He began by reading a line from classical music. I was overjoyed that my rituals contained music and poetry. When it was ended, I began to consider my next course of action. Gianiji was alone for a while, so I asked him if I might stay here for a few days. They questioned me, "Where are you from?" I claimed to have travelled from my house for many days. I had spent three days in a number of Gurdwaras. Come now to you. They began by stating, "It's okay, remain." Despite the fact that Gianiji had given me an inheritance, I was frightened since there was only one rupee in my wallet. I was living extremely simply, spending nothing for one day, two days, and three days. I was carrying a little bundle that was empty other than my two kurtas, two pyjamas, kachhira, towel, and sheet. After spreading a sheet and creating a cushion out of bales, one dozed out in the Gurdwara Sahib's hall. I was questioned by Giani ji if I had visited Langar. Giani ji, I don't have a house here, I said. My house is Guru's house. Once a day in the afternoon, they used to prepare their own langar. They used to store it in the same langar over night. Giani Ji had also saved some veggies and two parshadas for himself. They began explaining to me that we divide the parshadas equally between you and myself. Gianiji, this is not right, I remarked. One Parshad won't satisfy you completely. His age would be between 50 and 55, and his physique was a bit overweight. They advised you to eat a parshada and not worry about anything. Even though I wasn't hungry, I ate a parshada, thanked Guruji, and then I went to bed. Two or three admirers would arrive to pay respects in the morning because this Nanak Darbar had an evening show as was the usual. Giani ji stated, "There is a raga da wasa in your voice," when he approached me after the recitation in a lovely tone and rhythm. I pleaded with Giani Ji to instruct me in kirtan. You should sit with me, they began to say. In eight to ten days, he taught me how to play the tanpura and began tabla lessons with me. I used to sit with Giani ji everyday and give him full support. They were very happy, but my clothes were very dirty, because I had no money to bring soap. I could not wash clothes without soap. Giani ji understood my condition and provided oil, soap, paste and other necessary essentials. I used to recite the Sukhmani Sahib in the morning, and one day an elderly woman overheard me and informed other people about it. That elderly mother began bringing an additional 8–10 people. Given that it was a personal Gurudwara, Giani ji was overjoyed to see it. This Gur Nanak Durbar served as Bhai Gopal Singh Advocate's personal Gurdwara. No vertical management structure existed. The entire setup was under the control of Giani Gurdayal Singh alone. I used to sometimes obtain a shawl from the Sangat, which satisfied my little necessities. I used to read the Gurbani aloud. Giani ji would occasionally join me on the Akhand Path, which would earn me 10–12 rupees. With this Maya, I would spend a few enjoyable days, but this only occurred once every six months. There, too, my heart hurt. Nevertheless, I received a lot of respect and affection there. I never had anyone touch me. Living there was not problematic. Now Gianiji offered Langar, water as well. I used to give him a lot of assistance. I once memorised Rehras Sahib. I used to offer prayers and care for visitors. Everybody was delighted. I once asked Giani ji to help me since I thought my future was gloomy. What do you want, Giani ji questioned me? I said, "Giani ji, I don't understand this either, but I feel such a pain that stops me from staying anyplace. One day, Giani Ji and I prayed to Satguru together before we parted ways. I had a few coins in my pocket. I arrived at the Gurudwara after travelling to Nashik and saw the historical, old temple at Panchvati. I bowed and left because nobody was there. Tapoban is reportedly located along the Godavari River's banks. The hut used to be home to several sadhus who performed Japa Tapa (meditation). I simply went there. Between those cottages, an ashram was located. When I arrived, I noticed a sizable gathering. I discovered that everyone in this place eats in the afternoon, and I was also hungry. I was seated there as well. They were serving vegetables on two parshadas. I ate two parshads and drank water as a way of saying thank you to Akal Purakh. I asked a sadhu with a saffron obsession where Tapoban is after filling my tummy. That sadhu began advising me that I might reach Tapoban by leaving this hut. I left. Huts built of different chaparis were present. I travelled to the sadhus in several kutias. The sadhus were dressed in various saffron robes and came from various areas. They all knew Hindi. I learned that he resided in a hut after speaking with an Udasi sadhu in this manner. I told the sadhu that I wanted to sit here and perform tapas as well (meditation). I have to travel to Haridwar tomorrow, said the mournful sadhu. You may proceed, you will discover a cottage. Finally, I approached a sadhu in a hut and explained my situation. You may take the vacant booth in the corner, he added. You may reside there. A trust used to provide two parshadas and vegetables in these chaparis after midday. I continued to reflect on the Lord Mantra while I was there for three months. I would occasionally recite Bawan Akhari, Nauve Mahale Slokas, Siddh Gosti, Barhamah, and other verses, but my inner suffering prevented me from remaining even there. From there, I set off for Nashik Railway Station. I was sitting at the station thinking where I should go because I had no idea. No problem When a Maharashtrian Hindu saint came and began calling out to me, Swamiji, I was deep in concentration. I have no idea why he addressed me as Swamiji. I was simply dressed in a long, white robe and pyjamas, and I was holding a rosary. He began by asking, "Swamiji, will you come over and dine with us?" I was seated at the station in the morning. It was late in the day. I couldn't make up my mind what direction to travel in. It had passed midday. Once more, that Maharashtrian asked to have Maharaj come to our place for dinner. I don't know what force made me go with that man against my choice, but we walked together to his house. They cooked Marathi food at their home. In order to make parshadas, wheat and besan were combined. Vegetables were cooked with lentils and pumpkin. I expressed my gratitude to them and the Akal Purakh by eating. They brought a newborn infant who was eight to ten days old to me and requested me to look at his hand. Additionally, he pleaded with Swami ji to examine his hand and forecast his destiny. I protested that I had no astrological expertise. I stepped up and exclaimed, "The Guru should have pity and blessing," as he placed his hand on the child's head. Two and a half rupees were placed at my feet as the Hindu saint made a prostration. I folded my hands and slipped that Maya in my pocket before walking away."

Unfortunately, his dad's death in 1952 had to have a negative effect upon him and he began to feel depressed and cut off from the rest of the society. He thereafter left house and began studying the fundamental principles of Gurbani in numerous cities from numerous experts. He grew so absorbed in Gurbani that he quickly developed into a skilled speaker. After getting hitched to Bibi Sunder Kaur in 1958, he chosen to make Alwar his main residence.

Due to the precarious monetary situation, Giani Ji struggled mightily in the formative days of religious preaching to maintain his objective. He wasn't an individual who give up immediately. Maskeen Ji used to travel great distances to perform religious services and give religious lectures in cities and rural areas. His only means of livelihood was whatsoever the congregation utilised give out of generosity and love.. He bravely overcame all obstacles in his path and persisted in his mission to propagate the teachings of the noble Guru Granth Sahib for the good of all humanity. He chose to stay far aside from political issues and radicalism during his whole lifespan.

Maskeen Ji don't ever held back from urging Sikhs to embrace the correct administration structure, in accordance with the principles of sikh faith, to sustain the gurudwaras as well as other sikh institutions, no matter where he travelled in India or overseas for religious preaching. He just wrote a booklet on the topic of managing Gurudwaras. He felt extremely worried about the electoral process used to create the Gurudwara administration boards, a topic that is currently the main source of conflict between Sikhs all over the globe.

Giani Ji was really a titan who dominated modern-day Sikh culture for almost half century. He was a devoted Sikh preacher who was well known around the globe for his expertise, fervour, and dedication. He was a brave speaker who lectured with Gurbani and sikh faith related notions in mind. He was also quite forthright and reasonable in his thinking. He was among the handful of prominent figures in whom the Sikhs had respect. His command of the sacred books of Hindus, Muslims, Buddhists, and others permitted him to recite from them at whim. He was also an expert in Gurbani.

He was effective in spreading the Sikh master's teachings throughout North and South America, Europe, the Middle East, and Southeast Asia. His lectures were regularly attended and he had enormous popularity overseas. In addition, he founded a meditating centre in his native town of Alwar, Rajasthan, India, wherein every year on the occasion of Hollah Mohallah, intellectuals, speakers, and knowledgeable Sikhs gather for a function. He founded the Sikh School in Alwar, which has been quite successful.

His writings, that include several publications, cassette tapes, and Dvds, have influenced the Sikh society's philosophy and life style. Many millions of Sikhs and many others eagerly watched his daily speeches on the Guru Granth Sahib on the Nationwide Television channel, which were broadcast globally. Several an uncertain mind found comfort and direction in his lectures.

He usually set his yearly plans in order to move up and therefore always follow them no matter whatever. He had thoroughly studied Sri Guru Granth Sahib and had learned all therein included information on the Vedas and Bhagat Banis. He was fluent in Persian in addition to Gurmukhi and Hindi, and he frequently cited Bhai Nand Lal Ji. He also frequently quoted from the holy books of Hindu, Muslim, and other worldwide faiths throughout speeches, always included the necessary citations.

In his speeches, Maskeen ji frequently referred to Bhagat Banis, which is codified in the Guru Granth Sahib and frequently makes citations to Rama, Krishna, and some other Hindu deities. He also frequently stated that it is essential to possess a basic understanding of historical

Indian rituals and customs in order to comprehend the lesson of Gurbani. Nevertheless, several Sikh intellectuals misinterpreted his serious, logical comments as being pro-brahminical since they were unable to comprehend them.

If such "intellectuals" keep spreading these false ideas, it may even call into doubt the veracity of Bhagat Bani and any similarities to Islam and Hindus in the Guru Granth Sahib. It is said that if such opponents got their way, they may shout for the Guru Granth Sahib to be edited, excluding the identities of Ram, Allah, Rahim, and other important figures.

It simply serves to demonstrate how very little these so-called "intellectuals" understand the special qualities of the Guru Granth Sahib, the transcendence of its teachings, and the significance of its messages for all of humanity worldwide.

The sacred Guru Granth Sahib's teaching was propagated throughout the globe by Giani Sant Singh ji, especially in the US, UK, Canada, the Middle East, Thailand, and Singapore. Several people who weren't Sikhs also count among his supporters. He was quite proficient in English as well as Punjabi, Hindi, Urdu, and Persian.

Giani ji reportedly gave a Sikh head cleric a vow that he would visit Amritsar to perform spiritual lecture once a year around the time of Diwali, and he fulfilled that commitment for 25 years till his tragic demise.

The Jathedar of the Akal Takht summoned Maskeen ji to the Harmandir Sahib to conduct katha at the Sikh Panth's 300th anniversary event. Maskeen ji went to Amritsar to give the spiritual lecture regardless of the reality that he was at the time rehabilitating from a cardiac ailment in the US, going beyond the advice of his physicians.

For his contributions to humanity via the Gurbani teachings, he was given the honorary title of "Panth Rattan" by the Sikh world. On February 18, 2005, Maskeen Ji tragically died from a huge cardiac arrest while celebrating a wedding ceremony in Etawah, Uttar Pradesh, India.

The Giani Sant Singh Maskeen Ji talks have had a profoundly inspirational effect on me. I've learned the appropriate way for my spiritual journey through his talks. I clearly recall the day (18 February 2005), when my father gave me a lovely watch for my birthday in the evening and then very regrettably informed me that Maskeen Ji was no longer with us. When I learned of this news, I became really sad.

Printed by Libri Plureos GmbH in Hamburg,
Germany